MINDSET MAKEOVER

Bestselling author Steven Schuster has always been captivated by the intricacies of the human mind. From the echoing hallways of libraries to the serene landscapes of the Rocky Mountains, Steven has ventured far and wide in his relentless quest for knowledge and first-hand experience. Blending profound psychological insights with captivating storytelling, he has reached readers across the globe, igniting their passion for self-discovery.

MINDSET MAKEOVER

Tame Your Fears and Learn from Your Mistakes

STEVEN SCHUSTER

RUPA

Published by
Rupa Publications India Pvt. Ltd 2024
7/16, Ansari Road, Daryaganj
New Delhi 110002

Sales centres:
Bengaluru Chennai
Hyderabad Jaipur Kathmandu
Kolkata Mumbai Prayagraj

Published under arrangement with Dorottya Zita
Carlo through TLL Literary Agency

P-ISBN: 978-93-5520-947-4
E-ISBN: 978-93-5702-403-7

First impression 2024

10 9 8 7 6 5 4 3 2 1

Printed in India

Contents

Introduction

Sometimes the most common things surrounding us are the hardest to notice. We spend our days killing our brain, wondering about the great questions of life. Living life at full speed, we are too preoccupied reaching some goal, some expectation. We don't stop wondering about the platitudes of life. Although, doing it from time to time would improve the quality of our lives a lot.

Humans are thinking beings. This ability differentiates us from other species. We know that we think. Our cognitive habits develop more and more as we age. We learn from our parents. Later we attend school, university, we get a job, read lots of books, watch tons of movies, and connect with other people.

Each of these activities involuntarily influences our way of thinking. Cognitive experiences shape our view of the world. Everything that we've personally experienced goes through our own filter and becomes legit. Real. More real than the things we didn't experience. Even though what we believe might not be true all the time.

When I was a child, I spent a lot of time with my grandparents. My grandmother had very strict opinions about various aspects of life, and she was very vocal about them. She told me that people using face creams would end up with deep and numerous wrinkles at an early age. She also told me that I should never wear any kind of underwear but cotton ones because they are the only hygienic kind. She taught me to wash dishes, to set out clothes to dry in a particular way. I could go on and on.

Recently I noticed that the beliefs she instilled in me are still alive, and I am very defensive when someone contradicts them. I had a quarrel with my wife about what material underwear should be made of. I had a bad gut feeling when I bought my first anti-aging face cream, hearing my grandmother's voice echoing that my skin will look like the backside of an elephant soon enough.

I started reading scientific articles about all the "unquestionable truths" my grandmother told me. As it turned out, most of them were either outdated or genuinely wrong. I felt somewhat offended by the evidence showing me that I was wrong about so many things. And especially hurt that some raw, heartless science material contradicted my late grandmother, who gave me her best knowledge.

It's so much easier to believe what we hear from our loved ones. If you're like me, you hardly ever question them. You don't run to verify what your dad said about car engine malfunction. You don't contradict what your mother says about marriage management. You have a cognitive bias toward those who touch your *emotional mind.*

When it comes to accepting what foreigners say, there are two kinds of people: those who are skeptics to their very roots and who double-check each individual piece of information they heard, making sure that the source was accurate, and there are those who believe everything they hear. People are more inclined to believe information espoused by an expert, a professor, or famous people than they are to believe a "nobody."

Regardless of which group you belong in, you are positive your way of thinking is correct. This is just one out of many cognitive biases you have. You think a lot about the everyday information that needs processing, but you hardly ever think about *how you think*. And *how to think*. The moment you read this sentence your blood pressure probably rose a bit, and you said to yourself, "I know how to think. I have a college degree. I have a successful business. This is proof that I know how to think."

This happens with all of us. We process a lot of information. We accept it or reject it. Either way, it shapes our way of thinking. But what is our thinking made of? Why is it that the same concept can have totally different meanings for two people? Where do individual templates of beliefs come from? Are they hard-wired, genetic, or do they get their shape by absorbing cultural and environmental impulses? Can we change our beliefs? How can we become aware of our blind certainty instead of locking ourselves into a cell of close-mindedness?

The aim of this book is to help you detect the errors and cognitive biases you live with. I'm not entitled to tell you how to think, but I can explore with you what "thinking better" really means, show you the bushes your brain leads you into, and share with you a little mental clarity. I don't want to persuade you to change your thinking. I just want to help you achieve critical awareness about your certainties. Most of the things I accepted to be true without questioning turned out to be incorrect. I made lots of mistakes and had numerous quarrels and bad experiences until I got to this point.

This is the point where I admit I don't know that much. And in fact, even the things I know might be wrong. To prove my statement, here is a fact I accept subconsciously and which constantly shapes my reality—the world as I see it (and it's not only me; what I'm about to tell is true in your case, and in the case of seven billion other souls).

By default, individuals perceive that everything from the sun to other solar systems orbits around them. Everybody feels and thinks that they are the most important piece of flesh and bone ever. This belief makes sense considering that we live inside of our heads all the time and every experience we have from birth to death centers us as the main character. Everything we experience is about us.

We might think that we are free, wide-range

thinkers, but in reality, the unawareness rooted in our self-centeredness gives us tunnel vision. I'm not saying you're selfish. Or stupid. Or both. You're neither. The problem I just illustrated is more common than Star Wars fans. I had this tunnel vision, and in many aspects of life, I'm sure I still do. Knowing this, I would be the last one casting a stone at anyone who just had an "aha" moment reading my past few lines. I'm here to help you to slowly alter or lift the cognitive cataracts covering your eyes. Leaving the hard-wired, self-centered worldview behind can make you be more accepting, more open to the world, less stressed, and genuinely well-adjusted to life.

Let me tell you another cognitive platitude: The more educated people are, the greater danger they face to fall prey to overthinking. Smart people can come up with smart excuses and abstract explanations. They get lost in the past or future instead of paying attention on what's happening right now. And of course, they are convinced about their righteousness.

If you think, "I'm lucky that I'm not that smart," or "I'm smart and I find this statement insulting," you just fell into your own belief trap. You got caught up in the monologue inside your head that reflects your cognitive assurance. Stop reading for a moment. What are you thinking about? What chatter do you have inside your head? Whatever your mental gut reaction is, that's a forming element of your tunnel vision.

When I say "how to think better," I don't really mean adopting a totally new thinking paradigm. I mean learning to track and control what you think. To be aware of what you choose to pay attention to and what kind of meaning you attach to it. Paying attention to too many things, being inconsistent about their interpretation (believing grandma and ignoring the random old lady across the street), and unaware of your cognitive patters will make your adult life very hectic.

This is what the real mental habit makeover means. How to switch your default, hard-wired, self-centered perception of the world into a more opened, less self-centered universal awareness. This universal awareness starts where you admit that you're not really the center of the universe and you don't know as much as you think you do. I promise, these bold affirmations will make sense by the time you finish reading the book.

For now, let's just take a peek into the life of an average adult who knows that life isn't composed by bold ideas, wild adventures, and spontaneous highs, but mostly by routines, boredom, and predictability.

Regardless of what you do for a living, it will get dull eventually. An accountant or a whitewater rafting instructor can equally experience a sense of mundanity. They wake up in the morning and jog through their eight- to ten-hour workday. It doesn't matter if they take twelve cheering, this-is-the-time-of-our-lives groups down the wild waters, or obediently type numbers into a computer with a half-hour lunch break; they will still feel stressed and/or relieved when the errands end. Their jobs might be different, but the experience of having a job is the same. One jumps into his hippie Volkswagen bus while the other slides into their safe, practical, hybrid Volvo, and they head home to have a good dinner, kill time with some TV nonsense for a couple hours, and go to bed early because... well, they know exactly what tomorrow holds for them.

While they drive home listening to some hit on the radio, monotonically hitting the rhythm on the steering wheel, they recall that there will be no food at home since their wife went to visit her mother — again. Muttering some displeased lines about their fatigue and their wife's lack of consideration, they change route to hit a fast food restaurant. The traffic is horrible, as they expected it to be at rush hour. "*Why can't these people find something better to do than blocking my way to the life-giving Taco Bell?*" our accountant and whitewater rafting instructor both think.

They finally get to the fast food restaurant just to see it is more crowded than the roads because people with jobs and mother-visiting wives are all trying to feed themselves. "Why? Why now, why when I want to eat?" grumble the heroes of this story.

The restaurant is awfully loud, employing people who are slower than a rheumatic sloth. The menu seems confusing at this hour, and unfortunately, you're not the only one confused. People in line in front of you are also debating what to choose: Asian-style chicken for half-price, or the pork chops on full price, but double the serving size?

Why do you have to share the line with these other tired and confused people? The line is so long it's infuriating. Maybe you should go to another place.

But what's the guarantee that the line will be shorter there? Also, they might not have Asian chicken at half-price. So you decide to wait, debating on who you should take your anger out on: the cashier, who is more overworked than you and has a job with a level of meaninglessness you can't even conceive of, or the person who is pointing his meaty finger uncertainly at the pork meal while ordering the chicken one as if it is more healthy?

You start having mean thoughts to alleviate your frustration.

Some minutes later, which seemed as long as a lifetime on Earth, you get to place your order — Asian chicken — pick it up more swiftly than you would have assumed based on your low energy level, say a half-hearted, "Thanks, have a good one" to the cashier who gives you the "Are you serious?" look, which makes you regret squeezing out any kind of courtesy of yourself, and rush to the dirty parking lot. Back to the rush hour traffic, which you secretly hoped that dissolved by now since you spent a lifetime in the fast food restaurant. "*Nope, I'm not that lucky ... Not in this city. Not here.*"

You get home. The house is empty and the dishes are

not washed. You grumblingly take a fork and eat your Asian chicken from the box while watching some loud TV show. It has some funny moments, but mostly it is dull and vulgar. And the food isn't that good, either. It's getting late. You go brush your teeth, thinking about how meaningless this day was, then you hit the sack just to wake up at six in the morning again to repeat the same meaningless day.

Phew, writing about a routine day is even worse than living it. Day after day, month after month, people go through this hurdle. We all do. Everything becomes a routine eventually. It doesn't matter if you're an A-list actor or a janitor — the dullness of repeated actions will get you. Many meaningless routines will enter your life as you age. Everybody who has ever held a job knows what I'm talking about.

I know you wish to hear that these moments don't have to be dull necessarily and that there is a magical solution that eliminates the monotony of them. Nope. Sorry. I won't lie — some parts of our lives are meant to be dull and boring. I know that social media wants to sell you otherwise. Don't buy it. Our life is not constructed of unlimited highs only. But the point of my presentation on everyday monotony is to show you a different way of approaching it, rather than a way out of it. The latter is hardly possible, because everything becomes boring after a while. So does the most beautiful person on Earth, etc.

You can't change the natural flow of life, but you can change how you choose to interpret it.

The long lines and rush hours are those moments when you have to be very conscious about your thoughts. You can't change the challenging situations, but you can change your thoughts about them. You should, because these events poison literally each of your days if you let them. You can think that each traffic jam, each packed line is a global conspiracy to mess with you. You can take everyday events personally. It is very easy to do so, since you have an ingrained affinity for thinking that you're the center of the universe. You can think these events are solely about preventing you from being quick at the shop, making you even more tired and hindering you from getting home earlier. You can think others know that they are in your way and that they do it on purpose. They scream and select their meals awfully slow just to pull your leg.

You can be disgusted about the gigantic pork rib that dude eats, pushing his fingers deep into the meat, tearing it off the bone and munching loudly, all the while being totally oblivious about you still standing in the line being hungry. "*How dare he eat in front of me with that satisfied look on his face while I'm still hungry? He must do it on purpose to show off.*" When he finishes, you watch him rolling out to his oversized motorbike oozing of gas when he kicks the engine on. You watch him leave, shaking your head disapprovingly about his consumption habits. What a horrible vehicle owned by the most selfish, environmentally insensitive man. What an inconsiderate and pointless way of existence ...

The last few paragraphs were examples of the way of thinking that will surely make you feel bitter and miserable. This type of self-centered thinking makes so many people disappointed, pure haters of life. You can choose to think this way every day at the fast food lane or anywhere else. It is your decision.

But you can choose to think differently, too.

If you just recognized yourself in this introduction, don't worry. Each and every one of us thinks like this once in a while. This type of thinking is automatic. It is the cognitive manifestation of boredom, disappointment, and sense of meaninglessness. Aggressive thoughts like the ones above ease our frustration a little bit. But they create a different type of frustration. It is frustrating when life doesn't comply with our self-centered needs.

So what's the solution?

Change of perspective. You can think as described above. But you can choose to think differently, too. First you have to accept that you indeed *feel* you're the center of the universe, but choose to *know* that this is not true. It's difficult, and you won't always succeed in making this cognitive switch, but the more you practice, the better you'll become.

For example, you can choose to think that people queue in front of you to mess up your scarce hours of "freedom." Or you can choose to think that most of these people just finished a long, exhausting physical workday and they queue at the fast food line because of necessity, not because of choice. They can't afford a pricier place to eat. You, on the other hand, came here because it was close. Or the man munching pork ribs might not have had them for a year, and this was his special indulgence.

You can choose to think that everyone else in lines

and traffic jams feels exactly the same way as you do. They want to get home just as much as you do. That the cashier lady is not rude to embitter your day even more; she is just painfully tired after a twelve-hour shift where all she did was handle others' money and impatience.

Making this thought shift is not easy. And is never easy. Regardless of how much you've practiced thinking more compassionately and de-centering yourself from the universe, you'll still fall prey to impatience from time to time. Don't hate yourself for it. Just make sure to become aware of your thinking options. Know that you can think in a compassionate way or an egotistical way. Try to think compassionately as often as possible. Some days you won't be able to, while other days you won't want to.

However, once you experience how liberating compassionate thinking can be when facing everyday hurdles, you won't be so inclined to engage in trash thinking anymore. It gives you a sense of belonging. That you're not alone in your misery. Other people suffer just as much as you do — or even more. The point is not to find comfort in others' misery, but to alleviate your misery by thinking that you're not alone. If you're bold, you can try to ease others' misery too. That can provide you with even more satisfaction. Say something funny while you're waiting in line, compliment the cashier, or tell a stranger you hope they enjoy their meal. Don't expect anything in return. Just let out your frustrations in a constructive way and create rapport with others.

Maybe the man in a hurry in front of you is taking a favorite food to his deathly ill mother. Maybe the cashier lady works double shifts to support her three young kids. You can never know what others' motivations are for their hurry. One thing is for sure — they don't do it to upset you. If you take your righteousness for granted, you won't leave room for compassion.

The tricky thing about cognition is that where you give it power, that's where it will weaken you. For example, if you put too much thought into negative expectations, you'll constantly fear tragedies and unfortunate outcomes. If you use your thoughts to focus on money, you'll feel you'll never have enough. If you want to get a partner desperately, the longer the days will seem when you don't have one. Whatever you care too much about will eat you alive.

I know you know this and I didn't say anything new. But are you aware of this truth each day? Are you conscious about why you fear, let's say, aging? Or why are you so tight-fisted with money? Or stressed when someone stops you to ask a simple question? Most of the time you are unconscious about what you power with your thoughts. Your cognitive powers become cognitive habits. They become your default thinking settings.

Today these settings involve a lot of obsession with self-realization, money, look, and individualism. Don't get me wrong, these are important things, but they can imprison you in a very one-sided, frustrating, self-poisoning way of thinking.

You don't have to quit wishing for more money, or beauty, or smoother days to be more aware of others and the problems you share with them. You won't be prettier, wealthier, or quicker if you step on the self-importance of others just to validate your own.

Real cognitive power comes from discipline, awareness, and compassion. The other side of your "cognitive force" is unconsciousness, self-absorption, and the constant belief that the universe just wants to hurt you.

You can disapprove of what I just said in this introduction, or you can accept it. It is up to you. You can choose to ignore life platitudes, but they will surround you whether you choose to pay attention to them or not. Awareness doesn't cost a thing, but it can be the answer to so many questions in life. Changing your mental habits is not about changing the world, but rather accepting it and learning to feel good about it anyway.[1]

ONE

The deceptive brain

The idea of changing your thoughts presented in the introduction might have sounded like an easy thing to do. In practice, however, it is harder than it sounds. Why? Because there is another problem we thinking humans are unaware of. Namely that in most cases, it's not our thoughts which influence our actions, but our emotions.

There are two types of minds according to Zen teaching: the thinking mind and the observing mind. The first type is the voice in your head that relentlessly blabs, and even if you decide to shut it out, it still will project some pictures and thoughts. *"Heh, shut out? Me? Are you serious? You know there is no such think as complete silence blah blah."* The thinking mind never sleeps: it chatters to you when you queue (it's up to you to influence what kind of chatter will it have), when you're about to sleep, sometimes even in your sleep. Did you ever notice this? Spoiler alert, you did it with your observing mind.

The observing mind is the one you should use to keep track of your thoughts and actions. People don't use their observing minds too often. Even when they do, it's not a completely conscious action. I call the observing mind better judgment or my right mind. When someone cries out to you saying, "What were you thinking? You're not in your right mind!" that person actually means, "Hey, you! Please check with your thinking mind with your observing mind because it's running wild!"

When the thinking mind gets out of control, the observing mind can't do much about it. Have you ever asked someone for help how to channel your anger? "*What can I do to stop feeling angry?*"

The answer is, you can't stop it. Once the thinking mind gets unchained, that horse is gone. What you can do is to not relate to your emotions. Zen teaches that instead of telling yourself "I am angry" say "I feel anger." You are not the human form of anger. You just got poisoned by this emotion. Making this little thought switch, you'll defuse yourself from the emotion.

Why is it so difficult to make these changes of thoughts? Because they are related to emotions. We feel strongly. I could say we feel stronger than we think. Each of us, even those who claim to be rational, logical, left-brain dominant and so on. Why? Because this is how our biology is coded.[1]

The human brain consisted by the brain stem first. This small, snail looking body part is resided atop the spinal cord and is responsible for the metabolism of the organs. It also controls motion and different reactions. Hundreds of thousands of years later this little primitive brain was extended with the emotional centers. Thousands and thousands of years after the emotional centers, the neocortex, the thinking brain, evolved to their top.

I don't want to enter in neuropsychological details of the brain's construction. My goal with presenting the brain evolution timeline was to show that the emotional brain is millions of years older than the thinking mind. Emotional reactions, therefore, are more deeply imprinted in our nature than rational responses. In other words, the emotional center has a strong influence on the thinking brain. (Goleman, Daniel. Emotional Intelligence, pg. 10-12)

The emotional brain is much quicker to react. While the thinking brain comfortably analyses the situation, your emotional brain already responded to the situation. I said responded, not resolved. More often than not, our quick emotional responses get us into more trouble. When it comes to modern, cognitive problems at least. When it comes to questions of survival, our emotional brain can be very handy.

At the dawn of humanity, a responsive emotional brain was essential for survival. It was the emotional brain that had to decide if danger was around, and what kind of response had to be given. If you depended on the rational brain back then, which comfortably analyzed the situation, you might have died before the conclusion.

Another typical characteristic of the emotional mind is its strong sense of conviction that its decisions are correct.

Without certainty, your brain wouldn't send out alarm signals to all the nerves in your system to help you execute the fight-or-flight response. Emotional certainty, therefore, happens long before the thinking brain can even grasp what's going on. When you stay frozen, trying to rationalize why on Earth you said that ugly thing to your mother, and the only answer you can come up with is "I don't know," you're right. You don't *know*. You just *felt* like it.

The truth is that society developed and changed its norms much quicker than evolutional development could ever follow. We're still cavemen in some aspects, giving the emotional responses to today's problems that we did when buffalo attacks were a real concern. Today, most of the things we fear and react upon in a primitive way don't threaten our survival.

Paul Ekman was an American psychologist who discovered the relation of emotions to mimics. He also discovered that the high intensity of an emotion doesn't last more than a few seconds. For example, when you're so angry you could smash a stone wall, you should be quick about it, because a few seconds later that impulsive anger will decrease in power.

What you feel right after the swift appearance of an emotion is just a mood sustained by your mind. If the trigger of the emotion is sustained, you'll stay in a certain mood for much longer. Let's say you got angry that your spouse didn't take the trash out. The anger appeared in the moment of the realization. Everything that followed was just you grumbling about the trash for hours. You sustain your anger if you keep recalling the reason for it.

Sometimes people even re-evoke a bad emotion just to express their entitlement to reparations. Let's say you took the trash out yourself. During the day, you forgot about the garbage and your anger. When you faced your husband in the evening, you re-evoked your mood and started arguing.

It makes sense for emotions to only last a brief amount of time, Ekman says. If emotions lasted longer than the danger or pleasant surprise, people would lose focus on their ever-changing environment and might fail to react properly to a threat. Emotional hijacking can't be overcome or treated. It is an instinct. But you can be mindful about the actions that you take after the red or pink cloud is gone. You can decide to not sustain a mood after the first waves of the raw emotion are gone.

The emotional brain is very astute, though. It often deceives the thinking brain to help it sustain the mood generated by an emotion for a long time. The thinking brain can keep emotions present for a long time because our thoughts constantly re-trigger the emotion. For example, if you repeatedly think about how annoying people are in the line in front of you and how much you hate them, your frustration generated by the long queue won't ease.

In most cases, people can't influence what they feel and when they feel it, but with practice, they can choose their thoughts. Controlling one's thoughts will lead to better mood control. Emotions can't be prevented from invading the "right mind," but their effect and length can be reduced.

For example, if you feel that you have anger issues, pledging to stay away from anger and never fall prey to it is not a smart thing to do (even if some gurus tell you that's achievable). Anger will reappear in your life sooner or later. If you just focused on repressing it, the moment you feel angry again, you'll also feel you failed. You can't get rid of an emotion. But with patience and awareness, you can understand the emotion, why does it appear when it does, what triggers it, and what kind of thoughts can decrease its damage.

You have to accept that some emotions can't be eradicated from your life. Choose your battles wisely. Don't fight against the unchangeable. Focus on what you can change. You can start by paying attention to the *thoughts* that sustain your angry mood and intentionally replace them with another thought.

It won't be easy. In the beginning, the more you try to keep your mind away from some thoughts, the more intensively will they try to pop up. If you repeat to yourself, "I don't hate when I have to wait in the traffic jam," you'll still be thinking about the event that makes you pissed. Rather, repeat something unrelated, like this: "I'm going to have a fun evening with my kids tonight," or "I'll go to that all-you-can-eat sushi event on Saturday." The more unrelated the positive thought to your anger issue, the better. Drift as far as possible from the anger triggers. This exercise is a mild form of psychological conditioning. The brain can think about one thing at a time, and you're taking advantage of it.

This is the best exercise you can apply to alter your emotional state as quickly as possible. However, success is not guaranteed, even by performing this exercise. Some emotions are too strong, or you still are in the learning phase of thought control.

Even though the rational mind cannot decide what to feel, it can control the reactions you have to emotions. The emotional mind is raw and unselective, whereas the thinking brain fine-tunes its manifestations. For example, feeling you could kill your condescending boss is one thing, but you won't actually kill him. The thinking brain separates the good from the bad, the civilized responses from the barbaric ones. If your thinking brain can stop a murder, it can stop much smaller issues too. Just strengthen the thoughts you have as a reaction to your emotions.

The best you can do is to accept that you can never have complete control over your mind. You have a deeply instinctive emotional brain, which is imperceptible to social norms. This part of your brain will act and react unpredictably. If you become aware of this – presently uncontested – neuropsychological fact, you'll instantly become in a greater control. You're predictably irrational. There is hundreds of years of proof of it.

A few centuries ago astrologists believed that the Earth was in the center of the Universe and everything else revolved around it. Even before that, the myth circulated about the Earth being cube-shaped and having a clear end line somewhere in the misty oceans. (This is a myth but surely some people actually believed it.) People also thought that they could heal different diseases by cutting someone's arm and let it bleed.

When I was a child I believed spinach made me stronger but I resisted eating it to avoid getting disproportionately large forearms as Popeye did.

I believed that winning someone's attention and love was purchasable, so I bought stuff that made me "cool." As a fifteen-year-old, I thought it was lame to be nice to others and disinterest was the way to win others' respect.

When I had my first girlfriend, I thought we'd always be together. When she first cheated on me I thought that I would never forgive her. When we broke up, I was certain I'd never love anybody as much as I loved her – and nobody would love me as she did. Then I had another girlfriend who loved me much more than I did. I thought I was responsible for her feelings and I was guilty of not loving her more. I felt like a horrible person for this. I was wrong all the way through spinach to love.

I'm sure that if I look back five years from now to my thoughts on today, I might feel that I was wrong. I hope I will. It means that I'll know more and be better in five years. We're never completely right, though. Nor completely wrong. I don't believe there is absolute right or wrong. There are things you experience to be right or wrong for you based on your values. Neutrally approaching it, your freedom of practicing your rightness expands to the point where you violate someone else's freedom in doing so. Not considering extreme negative values that people consider right we can agree that "right" or "wrong" is subjective. Based on different experiences and values, people have different answers to the same questions, and none of these answers will be better or worse than the other.

Our own answers might be different today than what we thought ten years ago. Ten years ago I was convinced that I should be mean to gain respect. Today I believe I was wrong back then.

People have a history of being wrong about things

they believed to be right. You have a history of being wrong about things you believed to be right. According to these analogies, how can you be sure what you think someone else thinks to be right?

The brain is the deal-breaker part of our body that differentiates us from other species. It is, however, a very fickle organ. It makes us believe we heard things, it convinces us that we saw stuff that wasn't really there. It can even re-write our memory.

The emotional mind is associative. For example, when you fall and hurt yourself as a kid, that pain associated with heights burns into your emotional memory. The next time you go back to the place you fell from, or another relatively high spot, even if you're not threatened by falling, you'll feel some discomfort. You surely won't go to take a peek from the edge. This reaction is your emotional memory keeping you safe and away from danger. In this regard, your emotional memory is your superhero, always saving you.

The emotional memory stores psychological experiences too. If, let's say, you got cheated on in the past, it wouldn't be easy to trust another person again. Whenever you saw your significant other talking to someone of the opposite sex (or the same, depending on who you like), like Pavlov's dog salivating at the bell ring, you'd start building up an inexplicable anxiety because of your bad memories. If this emotion — a mixture of jealousy, fear of loss, and humiliation — wasn't extinguished right after it appeared, but rather fueled by negative thoughts, you'd end up lashing out at your partner. In the heat of the moment, you wouldn't even realize that your frustration's cause dates back to the period when you were cheated on, and that was what triggered the emotion. Emotional memory depends on its previous perceptions when it sends you a response, not on the current reality.

There are two types of emotional thinking, according to Goleman: categorical and personalized thinking.

Categorical thinking is the classic example of black and white thinking. "I'm the best" or "I'm the worst" — nothing in between. Living in the extremes burdens us with a high level of anxiety. It is hardly possible to live up to the expectations of categorical thinking, whether positive or negative. Try to minimize the use of words like "always," "never," "best," and "worst" in your everyday vocabulary.

People with personalized thinking take everything from criticism to neutral remarks personally. The table hit their toe, not vice versa. People fell silent just because they entered the room. Or worse, people surely laugh about them. Personalized thinkers are not necessarily narcissistic. Rather, they are suffering from a feeling of inadequacy. Fear of their own "imperfections" makes them take everything as a personal attack. It is possible that their emotional memory stored many events where they felt they were not good enough.

Personalized thinkers have selective memories, with a strong negativity bias. They are fishing for self-confirmatory memories in their rich negative memory arsenal to support a belief. For example, if someone has low confidence and they get criticized, they will search for memories that confirm the criticism — regardless of its accuracy. If they get a positive remark, they won't rest until they find at least ten negative memories that contradict the compliment.

Selective emotional memory, however, is typical for everybody who is in a charged emotional state. People are just hard to reason with if they are extremely happy, sad, or angry. Reason won't change temporary emotional convictions. In a highly emotional state, people have lots of reasons to support their own side. You know when the emotional brain chooses to react, the belief that it is the right thing to do must be strong.

Selective emotional memory is insensitive to time. If an event in your life is similar as one in the past when something bad happened, you'll give the same emotional response, even though the circumstances are now different. For example, if your opinion was repressed as a child, you won't easily speak your mind to your partner, even though he or she is really curious about what you think. It takes a lot of effort and talking to acknowledge the situation has changed. Your partner is not your parent. Also, you're not a child anymore. By taking baby steps, emotional memory can be overwritten with new memories. In these memories, people are curious about what you think. This process of memory change, however, takes time.

This is the psychological backstage of our mental habits. Sometimes we have no clue why we do or say certain things, while other times, we feel we're totally right. Question your thoughts and actions often, and don't believe everything your mind tells you. When you start questioning your thoughts, it means you reached a level of self-awareness not many people have. Make sure to question and criticize your thoughts in a constructive manner. You are not stupid, even if you realize you were wrong in something.

Daniel Goleman gives a short guidance in his book Emotional Intelligence on how to conduct your self-questioning as fairly as possible.

Be specific. When you decide to criticize yourself about something, don't extend the criticism to every flaw you have. Analyze only that one problem you wish to find answers for. Avoid categorical and personalized thinking. Choose a well-defined thought that needs questioning. For example: "I become overly invested in each fight I have with my father; therefore, I can't stay as level-headed as I want to be."

Don't blame or point fingers at yourself. The point of this practice is to understand where some emotion comes from and solve it, not to create new levels of self-hatred.

Don't try to kill two birds with one stone. Focus on

one emotional difficulty at a time, because each has a different emotional memory background. Taking your self-analysis out of context might make it impossible to find the reason of what triggered the emotion. If you don't know the reason, you can't substantially work on diminishing its effect. If you're tense around your father, focus only on this specific tension. Don't mix the thought with other events or people who make you tense. Daddy issues come from a different memory than road rage, annoying coworkers, or other events. Don't stack all the events that make you tense, because you'll end up thinking that you're a much more irritable, bad person than you actually are.

"Say exactly what the problem is, what's wrong with it, or how it makes you feel and what could be changed," advises Goleman.

Being specific is important as much for praise as it is for criticism, says Harry Levinson, a psychologist and expert on corporate and organizational behavior improvement. Unspecified or generalized praise can lead to false self-perception and overconfidence.

TWO

Neurotic vs. Psychotic

Today the word "neurotic" gets rather a bad name. When used in everyday language, neurotic has a negative, scornful, and deterring connotation. In psychology, on the other hand, a neurotic state describes a condition where the affected person experiences a lot of anxiety, poor functioning, and depressive inclinations revolving around their contact with reality. This psychological concept has to be distinguished from the concept of "psychosis" where people get separated from reality. Neurotics rarely represent a danger to society.

The term "borderline" of borderline personality

disorder actually refers to the conceptual separation line between neurotic and psychotic.[1]

After talking to many people during my coaching sessions, I realized that the distinction of these two psychological concepts (neurotic and psychotic) affords great relief to people. Since neurotic today has such a bad connotation, people tend to think that their anxiety issues are beyond help and there is something wrong with them (in some cases, this might be true; I recommend consulting with a psychologist when the problem of powerful neuroticism is a real issue instead of self-diagnosing. However, if you're just overreacting to some minor things, it does not mean you've lost your marbles).

There are two types of neurotic conditions, one referring to personality traits, the other to character adaptations.

The Five-Factor Model (FFM)

This personality traits model is based on the personality perception of the everyday language. The FFM theory is based on words rather than neuropsychological experiments. Patterns of thoughts, feelings, and actions belong here. These patterns get more and more hardwired as we age, and in adulthood, remain quite fixed. The theory separates five broad trait domains: openness to experience, conscientiousness, extraversion, agreeableness, and neuroticism. For easy memorizing, the five traits are listed as the acronym OCEAN.

One of the traits, as you can see, is neuroticism. Neuroticism stands for the sensitivity of the negative affect system. For example, if we describe someone as highly neurotic, we associate to him the following traits: overly anxious, a true worrier, irritable, emotionally misbalanced, reactive to stress.[2]

Each of the personality traits has two extreme attributives:

- openness to experience: inventive/curious or consistent/cautious
- conscientiousness: efficient/organized or easy-going/careless
- extraversion: outgoing/energetic or solitary/reserved
- agreeableness: friendly/compassionate or challenging/detached
- neuroticism: sensitive/nervous or secure/confident

Those who can't clearly define their tendency toward one of the characteristic pairs in each category are considered to be adaptable and reasonable. But they can also be perceived as calculating, uncanny, or meretricious.[3]

Character adaptations

Character adaptations are more situation-dependent ways people adapt to the environment. Neurotic here means that someone bases his adaptation strategies on his fears. The problem with fear-based coping strategies is that they rarely serve long-term benefits. They rather focus on momentary safety. In other words, people with neurotic character adaptations will choose not to go to college because they fear they are not smart enough. They choose to not ask the pretty girl or boy out on a date because they fear rejection. Unconscious neurotic character adaptation usually leads to self-sabotage.

In an article published in *Psychology Today*, Gregg Henriques, Ph. D. talks about a case he was supervising. This case finely illustrates neurotic character adaptation.

"Susan had just started dating Brian and she reported that on their third date, Brian was supposed to show up at seven. At 7:10 pm Susan called Brian on his cell, upset, asking him in a somewhat panicked voice, 'Where are you? Are you coming or not?' Here Susan's anxious-dependency needs drove her to reach out for contact and assurance. However, the response was 'neurotic' because the likely consequence was that her actions probably worked against her long-term goals. While Brian's response, 'I will be there in a minute' alleviated Susan's short-term anxiety, it is also likely that at some level Brian will register Susan as dependent and needy, which will increase the likely that he will actually avoid her in the future—which, of course, is exactly Susan's fear."[4]

The thing is, we are all a little bit neurotic when it comes to character adaptation. If you are stable in your relationships, you may overstress on money matters. If you are okay with taking risks in your financial life, you might be an anxiety bag when it comes to dealing with your overachiever dad. As I mentioned in the introduction, the things we power with thoughts the most (in other words, what we most care about) are those that make us the most anxious.

The most effective way of easing these neurotic patterns is to get aware of them, of their origin, and accept and change the thoughts related to them. Henriques warns about the importance of profound understanding when it comes to character adaptation neuroticism. Without real understanding, there is no real coping. He states that these neurotic patterns can be present in five areas of adaptation:

- habits
- relations
- emotions
- defenses
- beliefs

People engage in neurotic behaviors to ease their anxiety. But as we saw in the introduction, this behavioral method can only lead to even more stress.

The problem is that, carried out over the long-term, the habitual patterns are maladaptive — not only cognitive habits, but also neurotic actions. Binge eating is a great way to illustrate this maladaptation. Someone who is overly anxious about achievement, stressed about work or her relationships, can easily find comfort in eating. Short-term binge eating feels like medicine. Unfortunately, in the long-term it causes more problems and new things to be neurotic about like weight gain, health issues, self-hatred, etc. Compulsive cleaning, nail-biting, face-scratching, finger-poking, or the drinking of alcohol can also be a manifestation of neurotic character maladaptation.

When it comes to coping strategies, neurotic emotional patterns have two types: over-regulated and under-regulated. The former means that emotions are suppressed, while the latter means that emotions are over-expressed. These two types of coping strategies, if taken to excess, can become a dominant trait of someone's mindset. For example, people suffering with certain types of anxiety disorder tend to have an under-regulated coping strategy, meaning they feel the need to complain constantly. This way they can temporarily anesthetize their real or perceived problems. The other extreme consists of people who are always happy, never sad, and life is constantly wonderful to them. They probably have an over-regulated coping strategy; they never, or hardly ever, express how they truly feel. They keep their true feelings inside.

These two patterns, over-regulated and under-regulated, don't apply to everybody. Not every person belongs to one of these groups. These coping strategies arise when people adopt "rigid styles or express extreme interpersonal reactions in response to fears."[5]

At the end of the day, neurotic reactions are defense mechanisms that we engage in to decrease tension. Our defense system tries to set our peace of mind back to its safe place, even though many times this reaction does not truly benefit us. Two common defense mechanisms are rationalization and repression. These are quite harmful self-deceptions. Our minds play with our sense of reality.

Rationalization is the action when one comes up with smart and seemingly legit reasons why not to act on his real needs. Repression is the "exclusion of distressing memories, thoughts, or feelings from the conscious mind. These unwanted mental contents are pushed into the unconscious mind."[6]

Rationalization and repression can quickly become habits, and thus provide false beliefs about who you really are. Maladaptive explanations about how the world should function and how should you function in the world can lead to unhealthy self-image. Catastrophizing, self-hatred, perfectionism, and extreme beliefs are all consequences of maladaptation. Cognitive psychotherapy is a useful and effective tool to overcome these harmful beliefs, according to *Psychology Today*.

All of us develop more or less severe patterns of neuroticism. Don't be afraid of them, and don't think that something's wrong with you because you scratch your face or bite your nails. Think about what you feel insecure or anxious about when you catch yourself doing your "tic." Accept that whatever you do is not lame, awkward, or inhuman. If you trust someone well enough, open up about your problem. You can ask this person of trust if he or she considers you neurotic, or how he or she sees you from the outside. If you feel that you need professional advice, reach out to a specialist. There is no shame in it.

THREE

Neuroplasticity

Mental habit makeover in scientific terms is called neuroplasticity (you may have heard it referred to as brain plasticity or neural plasticity). The word itself is an umbrella term and "describes lasting change to the brain throughout an individual's life course."[1]

Neuroplasticity caught scientists' attention only in recent decades after research proved that cerebral aspects can be changed in adulthood as well. Previously it had been thought that brain cells developed only during a certain period of childhood and could not alter afterwards.

Apparently the brain has the ability to reorganize itself. It can form new neural connections at any stage of life. It can even heal itself, compensate for brain injuries, and readjust its activities to fit its new circumstances. This phenomenon is called "axonal sprouting." The undamaged axons of the neuron grow new nerve endings to reconnect the links of the damaged neurons. These axons can not only reconnect damaged neurons, but can also connect with other undamaged axons and form new neural pathways.[2]

Why did I choose to talk about neuroplasticity? Because this is the real, scientifically proven way to rewire you brain. Not only can internal, biological mechanisms trigger neuroplastic activity, but also your behavior, thoughts, emotions, and external environmental stimuli. This activity can significantly influence your health development, memory improvement (or deterioration), learning skills, and as you read previously, it can go as far as helping you recover from brain injuries.

Cells have the power to repair and recreate themselves. Brain cells are no exception. Human synaptic connections recreate themselves based on neural activity. Neurons that are activated simultaneously are likely to connect, and vice versa, the inactive or unevenly active neurons may not connect. To put it plainly, the more you use your brain, the more connected and active it stays. Today there is solid evidence that neurogenesis (the birth of brain cells) can persist even when we are old in the case of the hippocampus, olfactory bulb, and as some theorists say, even the cerebellum.[3]

Neuroplasticity also plays a major role in memory improvement theories and better learning techniques.

How can you take advantage of neuroplasticity in your everyday life to change your mental habits?

Using neuroplasticity to improve your cognition is not an easy process. It won't work if you repeat magic words in front of the mirror in the morning from seven to seven fifteen.

"Plasticity dials back 'ON' in adulthood when specific conditions that enable or trigger plasticity are met. 'What recent research has shown is that under the right circumstances, the power of brain plasticity can help adults' minds grow. Although certain brain machinery tends to decline with age, there are steps people can take to tap into plasticity and reinvigorate that machinery,' explains

Merzenich. These circumstances include focused attention, determination, hard work and maintaining overall brain health," Neuroscientist Dr. Sarah McKay says, quoting from Dr. Michael Merzenich's book, *Soft-Wired: How the New Science of Brain Plasticity Can Change Your Life.*[4]

Merzenich presents ten fundamental steps that one should comply with to reorganize and rewire his or her brain.

1. The moody brain

Your brain change depends on your mood. Or rather, it changes depending on your brain's mood. Or both of your moods. In other words, when you are in a focused, engaged, and motivated mood, your brain will release the necessary neurochemicals to make the brain changes happen. But when you're distracted or demotivated, your neuroplastic change will stay on stand-by mode.

1. More is more

The harder you try to change something, the better the brain change will be. Stay in the moment, focus on your task, try to learn with all your might and see that the brain will aid you to make an even bigger change. For example, if you learn a new language, put all your focus on that language. Deep learning is much more rewarding and provides a long-term memory.

That's why some people say that when you're not in the mood or you can't focus, it's better you don't even waste your time on trying to learn something. You'll learn much quicker and more efficiently if you concentrate all your brainpower into those hours when you're the most motivated and mentally active. Others, however, say that you should sit down to learn even if you aren't in the mood for it, and if you do it resiliently, somewhere in the process of learning you'll actually get into the mood.

I don't know which theory is correct, but I assume that both could work. Try them and see which works for you.

1. It's a numbers game

The more you practice something, the stronger and more numerous your neural connections will get. Strong connections are the deal-breakers in brain changes. The more you practice playing the piano, for example, the more connections are added to that neural activity (elements like movement and cognitive patterns). People say "repetition is the mother of knowledge" for a reason.

1. Synchronize

To increase the reliability of you neuroplastic activity, you have to keep your cell-to-cell cooperation synchronized. Merzenich gives an illustrative example to describe cell cooperation. He tells to imagine a stadium where thousands of people clap randomly. Total chaos. Then imagine the same amount of people clapping at the same time. Repeating a learning path helps with this coordination.

1. Associative flow

Due to practice and repetition, not only do connected actions strengthen, but the connections between neurons responsible for separate, successive actions strengthen as well. These connections help the brain predict possible next steps, which the author calls "associative flow." When you surf, for example, you paddle out, and when the wave comes you're getting ready to mount it. Thanks to the associative flow, the brain will know when to jump on the board, when to lean left or right, and so on. But you also use the associative flow when you're making your morning scrambled eggs. Without associative flow, our lives would be a series of separate, unconnected actions and a lot of stagnation between tasks.

1. Passing the trial of the brain

Here is another reason why repetition is so important in learning: because first-time changes in the brain are temporary. Whatever this change might be, it has to pass the "trial" of the brain. What I mean here is that the brain acknowledges the change but doesn't automatically accept it. First it makes sure that the new stimulus is good, useful, new, exciting, motivating, and safe enough to make the change permanent or not. The brain only accepts the stimulus as permanent if it satisfies at least one condition mentioned above.

1. Memory at work

The brain has the capacity for neuroplasticity if the

stimuli are coming from the inside just as much as if they are coming from the outside. In other words, personal interpretations recalled from your memory work just as well to trigger neuroplastic learning as any external change does. For example, if you want to become more confident in a situation, you don't have to score a touchdown physically in the moment, or win a competition. It is enough to recall these moments from your memory. Focus on these moments very sharply and voilà, neuroplastic learning gets activated.

1. The power of your memory

Whatever you learn gets stored in your memory. Your memory is responsible for helping you pick new learning topics and patterns based on your previous learning successes and failures. For example, if you tried learning something one way and it worked, the next time you'll try to learn something similar, your brain will pick the best learning method stored in your memory to aid you. Let's say you learn surfing. Your brain stores the best moments when you jumped on the board. Next time you try surfing, the brain fishes out your last best try as a base, and then incrementally adjusts to the current situation and gradually improves your last best try to a new best try (if you are focused and motivated enough as mentioned in bullet point 1 and 2).

1. On one hand you win, on the other you lose

Each time you use neuroplastic learning and focus heavily on mastering a skill, you'll strengthen those neural connections (as described in point 3 and 4). But at the same time, other neural connections will weaken. The brain does this on purpose to reduce the noise around the deep learning. It tries to help you by excluding disturbing or irrelevant cerebral activities.

1. Double-edged sword

Neuroplasticity is a double-edged sword. It can just as quickly and easily create negative changes as good ones. According to Merzenich, the older people are, the more easily they change their brains to the worse. The human brain is a "use it or lose it" tool. Without physical and cognitive training, cells (brain cells as well) start to atrophy and die. Cell reparation and replacement is organic until the age of forty. After that age, you need to make an extra effort in keeping you cells alive and healthy. If your brain stays inactive, it is very susceptible to neuroplastic impairment.

How can you use neuroplasticity to change some harmful or false beliefs?

To elaborate on this question, I will use the Four Step Theory developed by Dr. Jeffrey Schwartz to help people with obsessive-compulsive disorder. His four steps are very powerful brain reframing tools, but are quite easy to follow.

"Relabel: Identify your deceptive brain messages and the uncomfortable sensations, and call them what they really are."[5]

Let's say you believe that whenever you say something, people consider you stupid, laugh behind your back, etc. For example, you told a story to your colleagues five minutes ago and now they are laughing. You automatically assume that they are laughing about you. A sense of regret, embarrassment and shame washes through you following your conclusion. You become red as the Communist Manifesto and crawl to the restroom for an hour hoping that if you're out of sight, you'll be out of mind too. In the heat of the moment, you may call this negative brain message "reasonable intuition ..." But what is it in reality?

Do you have proof of your assumption? Is this fear real, or just a manifestation of your lack of confidence? Relabel this brain message and call it by its name: a fear-driven neurotic reaction. It only happens inside your head.

"Reframe: Change your perception of the importance of deceptive brain messages. Say why these thoughts, urges, and impulses keep bothering you—they are false brain messages (it's not me, it's just my brain)."

Now that you clarified what the false brain message is, it's time to reframe its importance. Even if it is true what you think, it doesn't change a bit who you are or what your values are. But considering that your defeatist thoughts are the brainchild of fear, the possibility of its validity is very low.

Why is this thought bothering you? Is it because you know you're lacking confidence? Because thoughts like this make you feel ashamed and inadequate? Why do you feel inadequate?

Dig deep into this question spiral and identify why

you really have discouraging thoughts. Deal with the root problems of your insecurity.

Your assumption that people are laughing at you five minutes after you left the conversation is a protective response from your brain. You have an irrational fear of public ridicule, so your brain is creating explanations. It's not you. It's your brain.

"Refocus: Direct your attention toward an activity or mental process that is wholesome and productive — even while the false and deceptive urges, thoughts, impulses, and sensations are still present and bothering you."

Find the main cause of your irrational fears and do something about it. Talk about it with your friends or a specialist. That's the long-term solution. The short-term solution is redirecting your brain to different thoughts. Even if your brain still suggests that your colleagues are laughing about you, force yourself to think that they are laughing about your boss who failed to see that some toilet paper stuck on his shoe —again — so he obliviously marched into his office dragging the white strip behind him. The more you practice this type of thought switch, the easier it will become to snap out of the fearful, shame-packed mood.

"Revalue: Clearly see the thoughts, urges, and impulses for what they are —sensations caused by deceptive brain messages that are not true and that have little to no value (they are something to dismiss, not focus on)."

By the time you get to this step, you'll know what deceptive brain messages truly are, and you'll know why you have them and how to break the cycle. It will be easy to see that they are nothing more and nothing less than brain chatter. Thoughts that have absolutely no value or consequence to your life unless you let them. The brain likes to blab, as you may know. Instead of focusing on its never-ending useless feedback, it's better to focus on the root causes of your fears and act to accept and heal them.

FOUR

Change Your Goal Mindset

It's Monday, the first day of a new month, your birthday, and the stars were shining especially bright last night, so you've decided this is the perfect moment to get the perfect body. You've procrastinated on this matter for quite a while, coming up with excuses like holiday season, a hectic job schedule, or a sick cat to delay the moment of starting a diet. But now you saw or heard something groundbreaking, and besides, it's Monday, the first day of the month...

So the time has come to become that flawless, lean, Lulu pants or biceps flashing shirt-wearing person you always dreamed of being. From now on, the street will be your catwalk, heads will turn after your graceful or bulky march, and Giorgio Armani will reach out to you on social media to beg you to promote his humble creations in your posts. *Okay, amigo, time to get back to earth. This all sounds cool, but what do you plan to do now?*

If you're like most people, you already have your diet carefully planned in your head from today to the day you'll reach your goal. You carefully selected a diet plan, the strictest of them all, and are starting it right away because you "*ain't like other losers who give it up after two weeks of painful fasting.*" You were born a fighter, so you'll fight. The *Rocky* soundtrack is echoing in your head as you start your badass diet. Day one, tick. Day two, tick. Whoa, two pounds gone! Mostly water, but who cares? Day eight, six pounds gone. If you continue at this speed, you'll reach your target weight quicker than expected.

Day twenty, nine pounds gone. Life feels miserable, weight loss slows down, you miss your dandy candies and soda at the end of each hard day. You're hungry and irritable. If only you could have a piece of chocolate. Just one. Just a little...

No! You remind yourself of your goal, your strength, and turning heads on the street. Rocky is silent in your head. Queen hums "The Show Must Go On" meekly somewhere very deep.

Some long months have passed and you've made it halfway in your weight loss endeavors. You feel like you've been drained of life essence. You look somewhat better now. Not catwalk good, but thirty pounds less than before. If you invest more time and at least the same effort, within a year you could – maybe, possibly but not surely – get your dream body. You go to work, trying to make peace with this thought. Later that day, your boss fires you and you feel that life sucks in a superlative sense and as you hysterically run out of your office, you spot a new McDonald's at the corner. Carmina Burana powerfully resounds in your head as you approach the wicked fast food chain.

Your proverbial angels try to stop you, but you eat them as appetizers. Without being very conscious about your actions, you order two large meals, a *diet Coke*, ice cream, and since it doesn't really make a difference, an apple pie too.

There were weeks when you didn't eat as many calories as with this one meal. Your stomach happily growls as it expands to accept all the long-desired sins you just shoveled down your throat. As the meal disappears, so do your dreams about having the beach body. You find comfort in the thirty pounds lost, but since you stop caring, the nasty weight sneaks back to your body before you know it.

There are not too many success stories in excessive weight loss. Maybe for a good reason. Most people approach diet as the necessary bad that helps lose pounds to within a certain timeframe. The sooner, the better. They starve themselves, become unpredictable and fickle, and any type of tragedy can deter them from their goal.

The other type of people, those few who actually reach their target, have a different mindset. They know that absolute denial of daily pleasures will drive them crazy at some point. They also know that they need a life-long lifestyle change instead of a short-term diet to preserve their good results.

These are the two mindsets of losing weight. People who stay fat want to lose weight to change their lives. People who get fit want to change their lives to lose weight.

Now you may wonder, why did I tell you all this?

Because it can help you understand what switch you should make in your mental habits regarding new habit creation and goal achievement.

What's the difference between goals and habits?

Let's answer this question with the two types of people presented in the example above.

The first type wants to lose weight quickly. He has a clear, strict, step-by-step path to success. He concentrates on staying disciplined and following his well-designed action plan. However, his goal is challenging, forced, and uncomfortable, with little progress, and does not take into consideration human factors like facing a hardship. He wants results, and he wants them quickly. He does a lot of work to eventually get his goal body.

But goals like starving yourself each day by living on 500 calories are forced and painful with little results and require tremendous amounts of effort and discipline. Sooner rather than later, the costs will outweigh the possible future benefits, your energy and motivation will run out, and you'll fall back to where you started, richer with a fresh experience of failure.

The second type of person focuses in creating new habits instead of pushing himself to the extremes for a goal. This type of person focuses on creating new life-long lifestyle habits. These habits eventually will stick, and when they do, achieving his goal will be effortless. Habits are automatic. This approach is not loud and doesn't sound as exciting as goals do. It delivers results in more slowly than a fancy "lose 50 pounds quickly" goal. But building new habits will help reach your goal with a better guarantee.

Goal setting sounds very motivating in the planning phase, but people lose enthusiasm after the implementation phase starts. Visualizing the clear outcome drowns our brain in frenzy, but it burns out quickly.

Habits are all about repetition; therefore, they seem boring. Habits, routines... ugh, who wants more of those? They are also more difficult to visualize. Close your eyes after you read this paragraph and try to visualize the following two things. One: You're sexy as hell, got the beach body, and you're marching down Broadway like a baller or Victoria's Secret model, Maseratis slowing down just so their drivers can stare at you, etc. Two: Visualize that you're doing exercise every second day from six to eight.

Which was easier and more satisfying to visualize? I'd bet on the first one. People don't like to daydream about routines; they daydream about highs. It is more satisfying to imagine having your dream body than eating salad for dinner every evening for the rest of your life. That's why most people who lose the weight gain it back later — because they saw their weight loss efforts as a goal, not as a habit.

In the story presented above, our hero got fired. What did he do? He turned back to his self-destructive habits. He was devastated, so his mind went on autopilot and started pushing him toward his old habits.

Now let's imagine that the same hero developed new health habits during the same amount of time he invested in dieting. He gets fired. What does he do? Something habitual. Only this time, his habits are better and don't sabotage his goal.

We can conclude that a goal-oriented mindset is primed to fall prey to unexpected changes. A habit-oriented mindset stays the same regardless of the circumstances. Goals are one-time things. Habits are endless.

I don't want to encourage you to not have goals. You should have them, but do not focus solely on their achievement. Do this instead: Acknowledge your goal. Then start introducing new, positive habits in your life that will make your goal happen for sure. In our example's case, instead of focusing on losing fifty pounds this year, make some key changes in your life: walk more, eat better, and play sports you like. All these new habits will bring you to your goal without exposing you to the yo-yo effect.

Keep in mind that goals will only bring you linear growth — if that. Habits, on the other hand, once acquired can result in exponential growth.

Let's consider weight loss. As a goal — optimally — following a weight loss plan will help you lose weight day by day. As a habit, adopting healthier nutritional habits will deliver you the weight loss plus improve your health, decrease the possibility of certain illnesses, improve your general wellbeing, and so on.

Short- or long-term?

Parkinson's Law says, "Work expands so as to fill the time available for its completion." In other words, if you give yourself a deadline of a month to finish a project, you'll take a month. If you give yourself a week, you'll take a week. This principle applies to goals, too. Surely, you can't lose weight quicker than biology allows, so that's not a good example here. But Parkinson's Law can be applied to diet questions.

Experts say that a person can adopt a habit in about thirty days. When it comes to goal-setting efficiency, it is much better to set a habit adoption goal with a length of thirty days than a longer timeframe.

A month is not that long. It doesn't take any particular struggle to do something every day for a month. For example, you could have a salad as dinner, or at the very least avoid carbs as side dish. So instead of your fried rice or French fries, cast your vote for the good old greens. Commit to this type of dinner for a month.

The success rate of sticking to veggies in the evening is much higher this way. If you instead planned to switch to salad dinners this year, you'd probably have the first salad dinner on December 31st.

The thirty-day habit challenges can be applied in every life area, not nutrition only. Hopefully by this point you see why it is better to focus on habit change instead of goal setting. Also, you can see why short-term works better than long-term when it comes to habit adoption.

Start small. Follow short-term monthly habit adoption plans. Focus on habits that have a better return rate — like we saw, eating healthier helps you with lots of things, not weight loss only. The more multi-functional the habits you adopt, the better outcome value you get from the time invested.

Based on the experience of experts and my own, I collected you three plus one habits that are worthy of your time and effort. I will try to keep these examples as unique as possible and not repeat the same stuff you can read in any old *Huff Post* article.

I'd like to start with the plus one. In fact, I already talked about it up to this point. This habit is the mental habit makeover from goal-oriented to habit-oriented mindset.

My number one life-changing habit (and that of many of my acquaintances) was cooking. I know, I promised weird habits, but you didn't see this one coming, did you? Let me summarize for you some of the benefits of this simple, everyday action.

You can cook whatever you like, however much you want, and you can flavor the food to your taste. If you're on a diet, you can make sure that it is almond milk that goes into your coffee, not trickster whole milk and so on.

Cooking is cheap. Or at least affordable. For sure more affordable than eating out. Unless you go to a super expensive restaurant where everything is organic, and low-carb — or so they say — your self-made meal will be much healthier than restaurant meal. Every small to medium business owner tries to cut his costs as much as possible. What can someone in the catering business cut costs on? Food. You'll get Signature Kitchen sausage in your hot dog instead of the high-quality, grass fed, farmer-made one, you can be sure about that.

You're right if you think that this tip almost equals the "healthy nutrition" cliché habit category. It is desperately important, that's why. You'll age slower and fend off illnesses like cardiovascular diseases, diabetes, cancers, heart problems, and obesity. You'll be sharper, more energetic, less depressed, you'll sleep better, and so on. Eating healthy is the alpha and omega of a good quality of life. And on the top of the quality food hierarchy stands the meal you made for yourself (if you take the time to learn about the best quality ingredients you can use).

Cooking alone can have therapeutic advantages. It's the same as gardening or cleaning. It just makes you focused on one thing and releases you from stress and destructive thoughts.

Cooking also opens the door to socializing. Cooking with your spouse, your kids, your parents, or your friends unfolds different levels of connection building.

This idea takes us to the second habit you should consider adopting. This habit is getting in touch more with your friends. Or getting friends if you don't have any. No, I'm serious.

We are social beings and we need company. Isolation and loneliness have never been so high as they are these days. Which is quite counterintuitive, considering that we can socialize easier than ever.

The amount of distractions also grew in the technology era. Our attention gets divided and the quality of our relationships has to suffer because of it. Good friendships need time and dedication to stay truly nurturing and satisfying.

Research has proven that loneliness makes you much more vulnerable to depression and physical illnesses.[1]

This world of hyper-connectivity has actually alienated true human relationships. I can relate to this, considering I travel a lot and all I can keep in touch with my friends with is my computer. But having a Skype call occasionally is not the same as face-to-face contact. Even my closest friendships don't offer me the same amount of care and closeness as they did when we were physically close. So I decided to make new friends while still keeping in virtual touch with the old ones.

After school is over, it's not so easy to make friends anymore. Is not like having a lemon soda after school, trashing the demanding math teacher, and forming those bonds instantly. You have to make a real effort to find and maintain friendships. Sure, social media helps, but don't rely only on that. Meet up with your friends for a drink or picnic at least once every two weeks. Everybody has jobs and kids and a life and a sick cat. But once in a while, having memorable experiences with other humans is necessary for a healthy life.

This habit is one of those, which have a compound effect on your life. When you socialize, you not only satisfy your need for company. You also improve your communication skills, listening skills, learn new things from the other person, practice how to be a better social being, etc. Thinking about what your friend told you improves your imagination. If you need to help your friend out, your problem-solving skills will be at practice. These are small matters, but they add up and inevitably make you a better person.

The third habit you should adopt is the good old "alone time." For one hour every day, do something you absolutely love. This can be anything. I usually read or jog. Jogging by the way, does not qualify as "my daily exercise," but my hobby. The fact that it moves me is just one of its compounded benefits.

If you like to chill when you're alone, I can recommend reading. The fact that you're reading this book already proves that you're a passionate reader.

Unless you lived under a giant rock in eternal darkness, you know the numerous benefits of reading. Reading nurtures your rational and creative mind as no other tool on this planet can. Reading expands your vocabulary, your knowledge, your imagination.

You can peek into other people's brains, and you can become anything you want through reading. You can understand other cultures and even glean a better understanding of your own.

Reading allows you to understand others better. Both psychology and fiction books can give you proper character descriptions and social skill development ideas.

Many thinkers, James Altucher among them, recommend reading four different types of books a day to broaden your perspective, knowledge, and interests. You don't have to read them for long. Give ten to twenty minutes for each book. If something doesn't entertain you, stop reading it. Don't force it and don't stay faithful to the "if you start something, finish it" slogan. There are so many books on this Earth that your life is too short to read even every book that suits your tastes.

If you're in the beginning of developing a reading habit, start with books that are truly exciting to you — fiction, adventure, biographies. You'll have time to read more heavy studies when reading becomes organic to you.

Just like Rome wasn't built in one day, your big goals won't be either. Life is a series of small goals twined in a chain. The chain goes on if it is backed by the proper habits.

What about career goals? What kind of goals should you set, and what type of habits should you adopt?

While searching for an answer to the question "should I pursue my passions in life?" I came across Cal Newport's book, *So Good They Can't Ignore You*. The main message of this book might seem counterintuitive at first. The writer says you should not pursue your passion. That's the fool's method. First I was stunned. *Why*?

"Steven, don't worry. I will explain everything," answered the echo of my patience on Cal Newport's voice. "What you should do is be okay with grinding a little bit, and when you grind in whatever industry you collect something called 'career capital.' When you have enough career capital, you can exchange it for whatever makes you satisfied in life. This, in some degree, can be creativity, freedom in your occupation, and a bigger impact. The basic message is that it is not the industry or the actual job itself that matters, but the freedom and approach you take with it."

The author assumes that human are thinking beings and won't choose an occupation they hate or are awful at. Everything you like (or can endure) and a little bit of basic knowledge multiplied with hard work can get you to Olympus. Passion comes from the accumulated knowledge, security, and success you collect by working hard in your actual job. The better you become at something, the more passionate you'll be about it, not the other way around.

If you feel you'd rather do something else than your current job, there is no point in being reckless. It's not smart to call your boss, give your two weeks' notice, and start chasing a dream, "a goal," without a plan. If your plan doesn't work out you could end up on the streets, and it will be miniscule consolation that you followed your calling. Instead set your goal of having a job you enjoy and start building useful habits around it, like deep work (you can read about it in the book *Deep Work* by the same author, Cal Newport). Or persistence. Or self-improvement. Get better at your current job to have career capital to exchange when the time comes to leave for good.

Who knows? By the time you'd be ready to leave your job, maybe you won't want to, because somewhere along building good working habits it became your passion and you reached your goal of having a job you enjoy.

FIVE

Meditation

For a long time, I was very skeptical about meditation. I couldn't meditate. I didn't understand the point of it since my mind was endlessly chattering. "Why can't you just shut up?" I cried to myself. Then another voice asked back, "Who? Me? I'm just listening. You're the one who's talking." "Who? Me?" Elaborating on this thought, I made myself aware that there's a voice in my head that talks. There is another part of me that listens to it. But which one am I? The talker or the listener? How is it possible that I hear myself without talking and I talk without opening my mouth? Questions flooded my mind. When I looked at the clock, it was one and a half hours later.

What the... Why? When did this happen? How? Somewhere between getting aware of my listening and talking self and differentiating them from each other, I fell into a cognitive trance, which was the closest I'd gotten to meditation until that point. I felt energized, my mind buzzing and relaxed at the same time.

I understood that meditation doesn't necessarily mean the absence of thoughts, but rather, prescind from them.

You don't have to be at a yoga class or humming in Tibet to meditate. You can do it anywhere, anytime. Getting the hang of it is difficult, but once you do, it will be the easiest mind shifting and shaping tool you've ever used. It is very healthy habit. Meditation has no negative consequence (unless you do it in your car while driving and you forget to brake). Studies and practitioners differ on the appropriate length of a daily meditation session. I think anywhere between ten minutes to an hour you can't go wrong with it.

This is the theory. In practice, it is really hard to still your mind and prescind from your chattering brain. Try to practice it just for a minute right now. It seems almost impossible, right? Now imagine doing it for fifteen minutes. No way... Doing it every day? Mission impossible.

Sometimes we know what we should do and what would benefit us, but there is an invisible resistance that pulls us away from the right path. This resistance keeps us from eating healthy, walking for an extra mile, telling someone you love them, or stopping an unhealthy habit. Practicing mediation is just the same. When you decide to try it, your mind will start acting as if it's having thought diarrhea and won't let you be.

"Do you think you'll be able to still your mind? You never do. You overthink everything all the time. Like yesterday, when you questioned Jane why she stayed out so late. Why did she, anyway? There was something weird in her reply. She usually is more talkative about her evenings. Maybe I should talk to her about this once more when she comes home. Or shall I call Jack? Well, what does Jack know about women, anyway? He has been married to his computer since I know him. Oh, how can he live without women in his life? Maybe he's the smart one. I mean, look at me. I'm stressing myself out when I should meditate. Jeez, look what this meditation does to me! Instead of stilling my mind, it makes room for more stupid thoughts. I should call my mom instead. Or watch *Game of Thrones*. I think the new episode just came out ..."

This discussion between yourself and yourself — or in other words, between your chattering and listening mind — is an endless radio program that runs inside your head on a daily basis without you being conscious about it.

Meditation can help you become aware of your unconscious mental activity, select the information that matters and has value, and prescind your ego from the rest. You are not your brain, and certainly not the garbage your brain projects as truth ninety percent of the time.

Do you remember what you read in the chapter about neuroplasticity? Learning something new takes a lot of focus, dedication, and repetition to maintain and strengthen the neural connections. Learning to meditate requires the same type of approach. The more control you seize over your mind, the more you'll be able to shift your thoughts from destructive to constructive. And that's the real life-changing magic. Your relationships, your mental and physical health, and your overall performance and self-worth will all be grateful for this new skill.

There is no right time or right place to meditate, but if you're a beginner, I'd recommend a very easy practice to get started. There is no point in making it harder for yourself.

Find a quiet spot in your house or in a park nearby. Sit down in a comfortable position. Make sure nothing is disturbing you. You don't want thoughts like, "Oh, that wretched rock is piercing my leg." Inhale. Exhale. Deeply. Repeat. Count your breaths. Count to ten. Then twenty. Then start counting the length of your breaths. Four to inhale. Four to exhale. Repeat. Still your mind. Don't focus on anything but your silent breathing. Do this for ten to fifteen minutes.

When you feel comfortable about breathing, exhale with a gentle hum. If you feel weird doing it, then don't, otherwise your mind will jump in with, "Look how stupid you sound." Maybe not your mind, but mine used to make fun of me with similar comments.

Next time you meditate (hopefully tomorrow), pay attention to your posture. When you sit, cross your legs — you know, as Turks do, not as models. If you can't cross your legs perfectly, don't worry. It doesn't have to look nice; it just has to be comfortable. Straighten you back. You can rest your arms on your knees or in your lap. You can stick your fingers together pointing upwards. This hand posture is similar to Italian communication, if you wonder what hand posture I'm talking about. But it is just as good if you casually rest your palms on your knees.

Exhale and drive out all the thoughts with this breath. Now inhale slowly. Feel the air spreading your ribcage going down into your stomach. Don't stretch your lungs only, but breathe into your belly. Deeply. Profoundly. Like little babies. They do belly breathing instinctively. It is the best type of breathing. It fills your body with oxygen and delivers air to the lowest parts of your lungs. Count to four or six while inhaling. Hold the air in for two seconds. Then gently, slowly exhale. Empty your belly first, then slowly push all the air out going upwards.

Don't worry or feel pissed if thoughts sneak back in. That's completely normal. Just start the counting again and strengthen your focus. If you allow room for frustration or anger, you've lost the battle. If you feel you became irreversibly frustrated, stop your meditation and resume it an hour later. There is no point in struggling to regain control while hating yourself. You will do more damage than good.

The breathing exercise is one of the most elementary forms of Zen meditation. It can take months to learn to do it properly. When I say properly, I mean to still your mind for an uninterrupted fifteen minutes.

If you wonder how meditation benefits you besides its spiritual value, I will surprise you. Studies using EEG and MRI machines proved that regular meditation indeed rewires neural pathways. It also increases gray matter. Sara Lazar from Harvard University conducted a major study to prove this in 2000. The Dalai Lama hand in hand with a neuroscientist from the University of Wisconsin, Richard Davidson, led an experiment to prove the beneficial aspects of meditation on the brain.[12]

The benefits of meditation above the psychological, biological, and spiritual are numerous.

It makes you physically healthier, as well. Your heart rate will stabilize, you'll sleep better, and your blood pressure will decrease too. [3] It will also reduce anxiety and stress in your life. Meditation calms your nerves if done properly. It also helps you gain clarity, be more self-aware, and have better short- and long-term memory.[4]

Meditation is a good habit, which has exponential benefits in your life. Besides everything I just mentioned in the previous paragraphs, it will bring other types of benefits to your life too, like being more patient and empathetic with people. You'll be well-balanced, harder to piss off, and more emotionally stable in general. Meditation is that magical card in your mental arsenal that can be of help for everything. It is like the joker in a card pack.

This doesn't mean that if you learn to meditate, all your problems will instantly be solved. You'll still have fears, past traumas, money issues — you name it — but your reaction and quality of managing them will improve.

All it takes to master the valuable skill of meditation is a short practice daily. As little as five minutes per day can be a good start. If you fear you couldn't be consistent enough, I recommend trying to learn the basics of meditation in a meditation group. On one hand, you can meet likeminded, nice people. On the other hand, you'll have the "I came all this way to do this" mindset, which will keep your mind more focused.

Meditation is one of the very few things constantly mentioned in self-help books that actually works and bears fruits with diligent and persistent practice. You have nothing to lose if you try it, but a lot to gain if you stick to it.

SIX

It's not about you

There is one brain fart we all experience in some areas of our lives. Some people do it in their relationships, some do it at their workplace, and some do it with their overbearing parent. Some in all the three categories.

This not-so-mysterious problem is that we take things personally. Did your fiancée just mention that he hates people who talk too much and don't say anything? Did you get vocal about his rudeness and added that if he hates *you* talking so much, you won't say anything ever again? In reality, his remark probably wasn't even about you.

Or when your mother cried out that she has so much work to do and nobody takes the trash out in this (ugly-word) house? Yeah, this one might include you as well. But for sure she doesn't mean that you are the laziest person on the planet who never does anything. That's just your additional thought.

In the introduction, I talked in length about how each event we experience includes us as the main character; therefore, we possess the unconscious belief that the entire universe orbits around us. Taking things personally is the direct consequence of this notion. The global economy conspired against your shares, the traffic jam occurred just to make you run late, the person in the queue in front of you is indecisive on purpose, etc. The list of examples is inexhaustible. This is why we think that each event involving us is about us — and every event in our lives is like that.

It isn't.

Sorry to say that but not everything is about you. In fact, if you knew how few of the things you experience, or of the people you think are talking about you, are really about you, you'd be offended. This statement is true in my case, too.

The more you learn to disconnect from your own

sense of importance, the calmer and more well-balanced you'll become. Don't take things so deeply personally. Let me share a secret with you: If you loosen your sense of self-importance, you won't become less important than you were. Neither will you become more important. In fact, nothing will change about you in the external world. But the world will change inside you.

It is very difficult to remind yourself constantly about not taking things personally, since it is hard-wired in your brain. You won't succeed all the time. But the more you succeed, the happier you'll become.

Keeping up this practice is much easier when you have to disconnect from negative things. It gives good vibes to believe that something bad happening is not about you. But if you want to stay fair and keep your ego in control, you have to do the same self-distancing from positive events, too. It is quite one sided to believe that only bad things are not about or because of you, right? At the end of the day, it's psychologically healthier to distance yourself from both good and bad events.

Why? Because while it feels uplifting to think that some positive global conspiracy happened because you're so fabulous, it will break your back to acknowledge a negative experience as your "fault." Still, you should. If you accept sunshine, accept the rain too. This kind of mentality, by the way, is an example of what not to do. If you make your self-worth dependent on such wildly fluctuating variables, you'll be very exposed to the chaotic moods of the universe. One day you'll be sky-high, while the next you'll be low as the Mariana Trench. When the sun shines, you're the fifth member of the Fantastic Four. When it's overcast, you're more miserable than Gollum losing the One Ring.

You'll become addicted to searching for highs, so you'll attribute every kind of positive event to yourself. And you'll be terrified of negative events, so you'll be even more sensitive to anything unpleasant.

What's the alternative of taking everything personal? Surprise, not taking everything personal. When something seems personal, like someone directly criticizing you, even that's not personal. Others' destructive criticism isn't about you; it is about them. Their fears. They took something personal. It is their issue. If you don't believe me, look about it this way: Why would people waste their time thinking about you when they have so much to think about themselves?

Your emotions are not you. Your thoughts are not you. You're not a failure. You're not angry. You failed. You feel anger. Make this little thought switch in your head.

There is an important part of the victim mentality. When people have a deep self-resentment, they tend to think they deserve whatever tragedy befalls upon them. For example, you told some horrible things to your spouse. The next day, your mother had a car accident. Even though you think that the universe did this to punish you, that's just your ego's imagination rooting itself in negative self-importance. Although both things feel horrible in their own way, there's no connection between them. Apologize to your spouse, visit your mother and appreciate her more, and forget that you deserved some kind of universal punishment for your meanness.

You don't believe it? Look at that crazy Norwegian guy who randomly shot seventy kids to death. Based on the universal punishment logic, by now he should be screaming in agony and facing a punishment similar to that of Prometheus. Instead he is thriving in his hotel room-like prison cell, constantly fighting for his release. And he'll be released, eventually.

You believe that he'll get his punishment in the afterlife? Sure. Let's say he will. And so will you for the horrible things you said to your spouse. In the afterlife. Not this life. Not by some universal conspiracy. You're not that important — sorry to say it so plainly. Your mother's accident is not your punishment. It is not your fault. Certain things just happen – good and bad ones.

On one hand, I know I offended you by taking away your sense of uniqueness. I was very offended too when I first got fostered by it. I started gasping so bewilderedly I almost needed a defibrillator. "*Wha-a-a... ?*" But then a strange calmness overtook me. Accepting that you're not that special is truly liberating. The thought can take so many burdening expectations off your shoulders.

Accepting your own place on Earth, which is not central but just as important as anyone else's, is one of the best mindset makeovers you can do for yourself.

SEVEN

Stop being faithful to your ideas

All my life from birth I heard things like, "Finish what you started, keep yourself to your word, have conviction in your beliefs." My grandparents, may they rest in peace, were the champions of ingrained, stubborn belief maintenance. When their beliefs were proven wrong, they still stuck to them. Even when they themselves discovered that their beliefs were mistaken, they still held onto them. Why? *"Because this is how we've done it all our lives."*

MY GRANDPARENTS BELONGED to that rare generation who witnessed and lived through socialism in a small, agricultural village counting five hundred inhabitants. Their beliefs adjusted to their circumstances, which were, well, lacking diversity and options.

BUT HIGH-ACHIEVING BUSINESSPEOPLE in New York have the same attitude when it comes to their beliefs. They just stubbornly persist sticking to them. It is a very typical human characteristic that when their beliefs are challenged, they hold onto them as Harry Potter to his glasses instead of going to take a laser surgery at the Muggles' hospital.

THE PROBLEM with beliefs is that they are not simple thoughts, but a part of our identity. Since I spent a lot of time with my grandparents in that little village, many of my core beliefs are the echoes of what they taught me. Today I know that most of these beliefs are narrow and simplified, at best. Still, when someone's attacking or contradicting them, or tries to make me waver in them, I become so defensive I could spit hellfire, even though I know the people who question my beliefs are right. I'm sure you can relate with this feeling.

. . .

WHEN SOMEONE QUESTIONS YOUR BELIEFS, it feels like they're questioning who you are as a person. It feels like someone else is trying to tell you what your real purpose is. This can evoke a series of negative emotions from rage to profound pain.

USUALLY WE HAVE four reactions to personality attacks:

- we are unaware that our beliefs are mistaken, so we fight back
- we are unaware that our beliefs are mistaken, so we choose to ignore the questioner
- we are aware that our beliefs are mistaken, but we fight back anyway
- we are aware that out beliefs are mistaken, but we choose to ignore the questioner

YOU MIGHT SAY this is silly. Or that only limited people would do something like this. Wrong.

JUST THINK ABOUT IT. There are so many people who refuse to believe that we actually made it to the moon. Or that climate change is real. Or who believe that Tupac and Michael Jackson are still alive, living happily somewhere in Fiji. Many of these people are not stupid or uneducated. Some of them have degrees from prestigious universities. They are not oblivious about these topics, but they choose not to believe in them. And no means no. It's like hard negotiation. Once someone takes a position, he sticks to it, and protects his stance as if his life depended on it.

PROPPING up an old belief against any kind of hostile, factual attack seems easier than saying, "I was wrong."

BELIEFS ARE NOT ONLY philosophical or related to something others taught us. They can be rooted inside of us. We carry lots of beliefs without checking their validity. For example, someone who was a fat kid may have difficulty seeing themselves as thin and fit, even after the weight is lost. People who have been rejected the first time they wanted to date might hold the belief that they are not good at dating, or not good enough in general.

KNOWING that the brain makes errors in its judgment, it is safe to say that we're often wrong about things in life. We are often wrong about things we're convinced we're right about.

WHAT CAN YOU DO?

THE BEST ANSWER to this question came from Derek Sivers, great thinker, best-selling author, and former entrepreneur. In his podcast with Tim Ferriss, he elaborated on a theory regarding beliefs and faithfulness in general.

. . .

HE SAID that we shouldn't be faithful to our beliefs. We shouldn't be faithful to anything but a handful of people we care about. We should leave reserve our rights to change our opinions whenever and as often as we wish. Although we may have thought something for sure yesterday, we shouldn't stick to that information if we get better information about it today just to remain consistent in other people's eyes.

WHO CARES?

WHO CARES that you told Aunt Mary you believe cotton is the best material to run in, but then you learned that some modern synthetic materials keep the skin in better health? Should you stick to cotton just because you were wrong? Nope.

WHAT IF YOU were convinced that you should invest your money in certain bonds, but then you got a better option? Should you keep your unerring image and invest in the wrong bonds or let others invest in them?

. . .

BELIEFS ARE all in your head. There is nothing else to do other than to make an intentional mind switch. There is no shame in improvement.

YOU HAVE the right to change your opinion and improve. And when it comes to internal (negative) beliefs, feel free to question them. Question them all the time. Were you a fat kid? So what? You're lucky you've lost the weight. You're not fat anymore. Get on the scale and see it for yourself.

IT IS FRIGHTENING to question your own beliefs, but you must do it at some point if you want to move forward instead of spinning in the same place. Do this simple practice:

THINK about your top five beliefs, some that you think are unquestionably true. Then question them. Go to the other side. If you truly think your beliefs are correct, you won't feel challenged by your line of questioning. If you think this exercise is bollocks and you don't need to question your beliefs, ask yourself why you aren't confident enough to do it.

. . .

QUESTIONING, feeling free to let go, and eventually changing beliefs is a powerful life improvement tool. Use it as often as you please.

EIGHT

The unknowable future

When we grow up life is predictable. As kids, we just comply with adults' expectations. We put our shoes back in place, we brush our teeth, do our homework, and come home before seven p.m. We have no income, so we depend on our parents' goodwill to get the stuff we want. Although it is not guaranteed that we get everything we want from them, for most of us, there is no crippling uncertainty in our lives.

But when we step into adulthood, this comfortable house of cards crumbles. As kids, we tend to think that we have so many problems, life is so unfair, every adult is so lame and neurotic, and when they talk about our problem-packed high school being the best years of our lives, we just boo them with disbelief. Then we blink twice, ten years have passed, and here we are dwelling in debt and working a fickle job we hate, constantly anxious about the future.

We're full of questions. What if the job we change to will be even worse than the one before? What if the person we decide to commit to will prove to be a bad choice? What ifs choke us. There is zero certainty in future expectations. Everything seems so risky. So what do we do?

Nothing.

We procrastinate, defer decisions, and avoid making mistakes by doing nothing. This avoidance protects us from pain most of the time, but also protects us from experiencing. Life becomes very predictable and routine like in most days, except when something bad happens which we're not prepared for and don't know how to act on. We enter in a state of panic and accumulate a lot of mistakes during our desperate attempt to fix our bubble. When the hardship finally ends, we shelter ourselves even more than before to avoid future hurdles.

Pain is helpful. Without pain, our species wouldn't

even exist. It doesn't matter if the pain is physical or emotional; it serves a very important purpose. The purpose of learning to survive. If burning our skin didn't hurt us, we'd walk into fire and perish in the flames. If we didn't know that tigers have the bad habit of eating us, we'd just walk obliviously in the jungle until we lost our heads — literally. If we didn't experience emotional pain from time to time, our personality wouldn't shape for the better. Some bad things should be experienced for the simple fact that they are useful.

Too much pain kills you, that's true. But too little kills you as well.

Besides, without a little excitement, what's the point of life? A little curiosity here, a little interest there. You don't have to be reckless to add a little buzz into your everyday life. Don't think about the future's unpredictability as something horrifying, but rather as something exciting. Fearing the future is rooted in one single evil, by the way: overgrown expectations.

If you expect to make a certain amount of money, or you expect to have the coolest girlfriend ever, of course you'll be filled with anxiety. The higher the standards, the lower the chance for success. Risk factor grows directly proportional to expectations. If you learn to lower your expectations, the unknowable future will seem less frightening. It still will be unknowable, but it won't feel risky or frightening anymore. If you succeed, good. If you don't succeed, also good. This mentality will bring some failures in your life, it will bring an equal amount or more of success.

There are some mental habits you can practice which will make future seem less scary.

The first habit is lowered expectations. Low expectations get a bad reputation today. "What? You have low expectations? You should have the highest expectations for your life because you deserve it. You are the most important person to yourself. Aim for the best possible out there." While some parts of the previous monologue make sense, most of it just puts unnecessary stress on you. Today's specialty mindset is one of the biggest obstacles in finding happiness.

Accept that you're unique and that you're entitled to different treatment, even if you "hate yourself," and then you'll think you are a unique, special victim. That's why you have high expectations. Because you believe the world should compensate you for your struggles. If you have a positive self-image sprinkled with a high sense of entitlement, you think you deserve the best things simply because you are... you. The world, however, doesn't comply with your individual sense of entitlement and overgrown expectations; therefore, you'll feel that your expectations are unmet all the time. And you'll feel miserable, and stressed about the future as a side-effect.

So I ask again: Is it worth having great expectations? Have a reasonable amount of expectation for the stuff you earn by doing something for it.

Another mental switch to handle anxiety about the future is to prepare for the worst. Nobody knows what the future holds, so it is a good idea to contemplate about the possible best and worst outcomes. You don't need to prepare mentally for the best case. If it happens, you'll be happy. Only worst-case scenarios need mental preparation. You don't have to get neurotic about it. Consider mental preparation for the worst as a cognitive insurance. You bought it, you have it. You don't have to check it every day, but if the worst thing happens, you'll have it.

Embrace minimalism, both mentally and environmentally. Many of us stress the most about our earthly belongings. Just like in the case of high expectations, the more you have, the more you fear to lose. Own the necessary. As little as possible. Stuff won't make you happy, anyway. As Derek Sivers said, "Own less, depend on even less."

Accept that failures, tragedies, and disasters are inevitable. Expect them. They will come. I know you hate me now for this. You'd rather hear something like, "With the power of the law of attraction, you can avoid bad things if you focus on happy things." Yes. Sure. And I just took Santa out for a barbecue party. He didn't like the meat; he said beef was too chewy. He prefers wild game.

Just think about your idols. Every successful person has a story of "and then the worst happened." Bad stories don't define our futures, but they can come anytime. You don't have to panic; just be prepared. Don't stick your head in the sand.

Don't take your health, family, money, or freedom for granted. You'll see how much more you'll appreciate each of them if you acknowledge that they can be gone in the next moment.

Leave the door opened for opportunities. The future

is less frightening if you know you have options if plan A fails. For example, if you buy a house you get a sense of ownership, but it leaves you without the chance to move if you change your mind about it.

Don't make inflexible plans. Since you don't know what the future holds, or what will you want in five years, making ironclad plans for the future is unnecessarily stressful. Have an idea of what you want today, but leave options open for your future self to decide about when the time comes.

NINE

Accept that you're average

My teenage daughter has been very excited about the movie *Wonder Woman*. You know, first real woman superhero movie, Gal Gadot, Israeli bombshell, fine trailer. Bought the ticket in advance for the premier, munched on her popcorn half an hour before the movie even started in the back row like a boss.

The movie was amazing, and by the time it ended, she was flooded with a sense of superiority. "Behold, world, here I come, a real-life wonder woman. I'm like Batman, Superman, and Hulk forged into one person (I know not all of these are DC characters). My strength is multiplied now with the worth of a large popcorn, and I'll destroy anyone who tells me they are carbs," she told me jokingly.

Why is the character of Wonder Woman or any other superhero so intriguing? Because they impersonate everything we want to be. They have infinite power, exquisite beauty, they are often mega-rich or smart as Einstein. Often both. They win in the end. If they don't, it means there's a sequel coming. They have minor vulnerabilities, but that makes them even more likable. They're badass drivers and fight like Bruce Lee and Leonidas melted into one. And yes. They don't exist.

Each human era had its superhero concept they could worship and hope to be like. Starting from cavemen's nature deity concepts to Wolverine from *The X-Men,* people kept their superhuman concepts trendy and updated. Some eras were more realistic — for example, knights in the Middle Ages fighting for God and beauty. And some were less realistic, like when Hercules was slaying every mythical creature he encountered.

Heroes represent power, justice, and perfection. They are unwaveringly righteous no matter what.

They are everything we are not. Why did we need them from the very beginning?

Do these figures give hope for everyday mortals? Do they help to cope with your own powerlessness, and flawed character?

Everybody wants to feel special, to make a change in the world, and to secure an undying legacy in history books. Still, not more than a couple thousand of people actually succeed in this endeavor. What about the rest of us? The remaining 7.2 billion? Of course we need something to cling to that gives us hope that we'll be one of that couple thousand real deals.

When you daydream about your future success, your often picture it as a rosy transition from rookie to rock star that involves a lot of joy, occasional graceful failures making you more respectful, and high-fiving hundreds of people at a stadium in which you're performing the best show of your life.

But in reality, great successes are usually triggered by trauma or an extreme negative event in one's life — losing your income source, a divorce, a failed business, or the death of a loved one. Trauma and failure force you to slow down in whatever you're doing, take a step back, and contemplate your deepest values and motivations in life. In the best case, after a big fall, you get yourself together and put your head to some real work. In the worst case, you dig yourself even deeper in misery.

Let's be optimistic here and say you put all your best effort in achieving your goal. You gracefully fail and be reborn as a phoenix, becoming two times stronger at the break lines. You face all the traumas, fight all the odds that are between you and your dreams, and the hardship of life doesn't get you. Still, against all your best efforts and heroism, the best you can achieve is a mediocre result.

Why? Because like it or not, most of us was not born to be exceptional — regardless of what does today's go-for-it, get-it, if-you-can-dream-it-you-can-do-it culture shoves down on our throats. This sounds counterintuitive and depressing, but let me elaborate on the thought and you'll see it is not so bad.

If you paid even minimal attention to statistic class at school (and you survived it with a sane mind), you might have heard of the bell curve. The bell curve is a bell-shaped, convex curve on a graph (I'm not sure if I helped or confused you with this description). Let's put all seven billion people on the vertical side of the graph, and below-average, average, and above-average characteristics on the horizontal side.

On the ascending twenty percent of the curve are the people who have below-average skills at a random craft — let's say painting. On the descending twenty percent of the curve are the people who have above-average painting skills. In the mid-section, sixty percent of the bell curve are people who are average at painting.

Let's pick a painter — let's say Picasso (my favorite). He was a painting genius. If I had to position him on our imaginary bell curve of painting skills, he'd be somewhere at the very tip of the right, descending side, in the top one percent of people with above-average painting skills. Now imagine a person struggling to sketch a stick man. Probably a blind dog could draw a better picture, but certainly most of us would. We are all mesmerized by the legacy of Picasso and we laugh about the person whose amorphous humanoid drawing is probably the best of his life. The truth is, we'll probably never be either of them.

We all have strengths and weaknesses. But at the end of the day, most of us are quite average at most things we do. And that's perfectly fine. Nobody aims for mediocrity — which is good. I would never encourage you to not try becoming the best version of yourself. Trying to get ahead in life having mediocre goals won't challenge you enough. But accepting a mediocre result is okay.

There are so few of us who are willing to accept this. People revolt, they start dwelling in their offended ego, screaming about how special they are, how much they deserve excellence. But to become above-average at something, you have to invest a lot of time and energy into it. Even to excel at one thing might take a lifetime. And because we are limited in time and energy, only some people will be really outstanding at more than one thing, if anything at all. For each Picasso, Dostoyevsky, and Michael Phelps, there are hundreds of millions of... us. Regardless of how we grind, some of us won't get there. This doesn't mean that our life is worthless or will lack happiness. In fact, this means we are normal human beings.

It takes courage and awareness to realize our own mediocrity. Realizing it doesn't mean that we should give up on our dreams. Nobody knows who will be the lucky upper twenty percent. We should strive to be our best selves each day, go for what we dream, fight and win and laugh and cry and be okay with our mediocrity.

I know it has never been harder to be okay with mediocrity than today. Technology and social media culture exposes us to unrealistic expectations. Everything memorable we read about or see presents the extremes of the bell curve. Why? Because extreme good and extreme bad are attention grabbing.

Attention, however, is limited. So only those things that are exceptionally good or bad leak into our brains — the best models, the best diet, the best car, the funniest people, the richest ones, etc. As a consequence, our sense of reality got so distorted that we started to believe that real life is about those extremes, when real life happens in the sixty percent of the bell curve.

Once I was fantasizing to make a script for a movie that presents a couple's life after the big romance part — a movie that would show the regular, everyday life of people who love each other and have no problems apart from the regular ones. No young blonde in the picture, no tripods invading the earth, no daughter getting kidnapped. Just an average life. My argument for this movie was to show a good example of relationships to the generation that grew up on Disney and *Titanic*. When I presented my idea to my wife, she promptly talked me out of it by saying, "No one would buy or watch such a movie. No one cares about average."

She's right – as always. No one does. Even though our lives, and the lives of the celebrities we follow on social media are composed of mostly average events. Still, since our attention is constantly grabbed by extraordinary events, we ended up believing that is the new normal. Therefore, anytime when we're not experiencing exceptional circumstances (99.9 percent of the time), we end up thinking something's wrong with us. We start feeling insecure about ourselves. We feel pressure to prove our specialness. Some of us try to get mega-rich, while others try excelling with their knowledge or physical abilities. Sometimes, people reach out to the dark side and try excelling by doing crazy stuff like killing people. The main aim is to be different than the rest of society, no matter what. This is a psychological byproduct of our society today, and it is not a good one.

The cruelest aspect of today's exceptionalism is that even exceptional people are totally forgettable. Some practice their craft for long years, investing a lot of money and hours to capture their excellence on a camera to show the world. You get those five seconds of exhilaration when you watch the video, and five minutes later, you're hooked on the next amazing thing. For example, you can watch a professional surfer flawlessly riding a huge wave and start feeling jealous, thinking, "Oh, that's so cool. I'd never be able to do that." Then, supporting your head with one hand, you scroll down on your Reddit feed and you stumble upon another video about a bear tamer who makes the bear jump and dance. By this moment, the surfer is long forgotten.

As you can see, there is a competition even in the field of excellence. While individually, the surfer and the bear tamer do some amazingly unique stuff, being thrown together into the deep ocean of the internet, their performance becomes average. This is the biggest contradiction of the everybody-can-become-excellent concept. If everybody is excelling, nobody is.

People fear to accept mediocrity because they believe that's the highway to living an unsuccessful and sad life. There are some hidden problems in thoughts like this. Namely, if you think that only an exceptional life is a worthy life, you basically consider most people's lives unworthy. Think about it — is that really true? Are people's lives unworthy, sad, and boring just because they don't win the Super Bowl every day?

Don't worry accepting that your (mine and everybody's) life is mostly mediocre. People who reach the above-average level of excellence are also average people, just focused. They don't think they are that special; they just get obsessed with something deeper than the rest of us and are willing to devote their life to that purpose. What you can't see on social media is that they hardly ever go out for a beer with friends. They eat protein bars and weird food every day. They train and practice when you're watching Netflix and sipping beer. True achievers constantly feel they are average or below-average — this notion pushes them to improve more and more.

Let me tell you a secret: As soon as you take a deep breath, gather the courage to tell yourself, "Yes, I'm average, but that's just normal and I'm still worthy and capable of a happy life," a lot of pressure will leave your system. You'll get rid of that excruciating compulsion to become more and more for the sake of putting on a show. You'll accept who you are and focus on being the best version of yourself. And while focusing on your own stuff, striving to be better than the day before, you might peak in some areas and get those fifteen minutes of exceptionalism you crave. When you walk toward your goal because it gives you pleasure instead of being dragged by expectations, you'll feel much happier and fulfilled, regardless of the outcome.

Slowly, you'll learn to appreciate those proverbial small things in life like the security of a good friendship, making someone happy, helping a person in need, laughing with your love, reading something exciting, or eating a great Italian gelato. All these events are what we consider "average," and yet life makes the most sense during these moments.

When you ever think about finding a shortcut, an excuse or an exceptional moment you can share, remember: life is in the messy details.

Final Thoughts

Mindset makeover means finding a deeper reason for your existence than superficial goals, compliance with the trends, or striving to specialty. Find something to chase doesn't have a definitive ending point. Otherwise, as soon as you reach the goal it will leave your life empty and directionless.

Some world famous athletes are comfortable when their careers end and they retire with grace. Others end up on Dancing with the Stars. It is not a coincidence that the athletes who are motivated to achieve success for a greater good than their own fame handle their post-career period much better. Those who work to help starving children in their country, or to build a business that serves the common good are much more fulfilled than who only wish to enrich themselves. People who have a greater cause than themselves remain content even after their goals are achieved.

I followed the 2016 CrossFit Games closely. In the individual female group, there were two possible candidates for the gold medal – the Icelandic Katrin Davidsdottir and the Australian Tia Toomey. Both women worked extremely hard to prove themselves during the three days of the Games. They were equally matched in almost every aspect. The only difference between them was their motivation for the title. While Tia Toomey was grinding for the medal and to finally be able to call herself a CrossFit champion, Katrin competed in the memory of her recently deceased grandmother who used to be her greatest supporter. Beneath Katrin's stamina, there was an extra motivator: love, which burns much stronger than the motivation for fame. Katrin won the title in 2016. Tia Toomey lost by only seven points.

In 2017 Tia Toomey won the championship. Besides working even harder than before, she had a mentality shift – she just wanted to become the best version of herself instead of besting others.

However, meaning in life doesn't always have to be grandiose. Sometimes small things give greater meaning than any Earth-shifting idea. For example, I sat down to finish my book while hungry. While the chicken was peacefully getting ready in the slow cooker, I thought about how to leave a final message to you. I promised myself I wouldn't eat until I finished these final paragraphs, which gives some additional importance to the food.

And then something hit me. I don't have to find the greatest takeaway in the world to make this book valuable. That would have my falling into the folly of Tia Toomey – and acting contrary to this book's message. So I got up to check the condition of the chicken and fetch myself a plate. What's more, I prepared one for my wife and son because I assume they are hungry. By this simple act, I made the world a better place for three human beings at once.

Sometimes there is magic in a simple act. Sometimes it is enough to make your family smile and find happiness in it. Sometimes the present meaning of life is a chicken stew with fresh vegetables.

If you wanted to make the world a better place in this moment, what would you do?

Good luck!

Steve

Reference

Asatryan, Kira. *4 Disorders That May Thrive on Loneliness.* Psychology Today. 2015.

https://www.psychologytoday.com/blog/the-art-closeness/201507/4-disorders-may-thrive-loneliness

Hampton, Debbie. *Neuroplasticity: The 10 Fundamentals Of Rewiring Your Brain.* Reset. 2015. http://reset.me/story/neuroplasticity-the-10-fundamentals-of-rewiring-your-brain/

Henriques, Gregg Ph.D. *(When) Are You Neurotic?* Psychology Today. 2012.

https://www.psychologytoday.com/blog/theory-knowledge/201211/when-are-you-neurotic

Kok, B. E., Waugh, C. E., & Fredrickson, B. L. *Meditation and health: The search for mechanisms of action. Social and Personality Psychology Compass,* 7(1), 27–39. 2013.

Lazar, S. W., Kerr, C. E., Wasserman, R. H., Gray, J. R., Greve, D. N., Treadway, M. T., Benson, H. *Meditation experience is associated with increased cortical thickness.* Neuroreport, 16(17), 1893. 2005.

Livingston R.B. *Brain mechanisms in conditioning and learning.* Neurosciences Research Program Bulletin. Pg. 349–354. 1966.

Lutz, A.; Greischar, L.L.; Rawlings, N.B.; Ricard, M.; Davidson, R. J. *Long-term meditators self-induce high-amplitude gamma synchrony during mental practice.* PNAS. 101 (46): 16369–73. PMC 526201Freely accessible. 2004.

McKey, Zoe. *Discipline Your Mind.* CreateSpace Independent Publishing. 2017

MediciNet. *Medical Definition of Neuroplasticity.* MediciNet. 2017.

http://www.medicinenet.com/script/main/art.asp?articlekey=40362

Rakic, P. *Neurogenesis in adult primate neocortex: an evaluation of the evidence.* Nature Reviews Neuroscience. 3 (1): 65–71. 2002.

Schwartz, Jeffrey. MD. *You Are Not Your Brain.* Avery. 2011.

Toegel, G.; Barsoux, J. L. *How to become a better leader*. MIT Sloan Management Review. 53 (3): 51–60. 2012.

The Editors of Encyclopædia Britannica. *Repression.* Britannica.

https://www.britannica.com/topic/repression-psychology

Zeidan, F., Johnson, S. K., Diamond, B. J., David, Z., & Goolkasian, P. *Mindfulness meditation improves cognition: Evidence of brief mental training.* 2010.

Notes

Introduction

1. This introduction was inspired by David Foster Wallace's commencement speech at Kenyon Collage in 2005.

1. The deceptive brain

1. McKey, Zoe. *Discipline Your Mind.* CreateSpace Independent Publishing. 2017

2. Neurotic vs. Psychotic

1. Henriques, Gregg Ph.D. *(When) Are You Neurotic?* Psychology Today. 2012. https://www.psychologytoday.com/blog/theory-knowledge/201211/when-are-you-neurotic
2. Henriques, Gregg Ph.D. *(When) Are You Neurotic?* Psychology Today. 2012. https://www.psychologytoday.com/blog/theory-knowledge/201211/when-are-you-neurotic
3. Toegel, G.; Barsoux, J. L. *How to become a better leader.* MIT Sloan Management Review. 53 (3): 51–60. 2012.
4. Henriques, Gregg Ph.D. *(When) Are You Neurotic?* Psychology Today. 2012. https://www.psychologytoday.

com/blog/theory-knowledge/201211/when-are-you-neurotic

5. Henriques, Gregg Ph.D. *(When) Are You Neurotic?* Psychology Today. 2012. https://www.psychologytoday.com/blog/theory-knowledge/201211/when-are-you-neurotic
6. The Editors of Encyclopædia Britannica. *Repression.* Britannica. https://www.britannica.com/topic/repression-psychology

3. Neuroplasticity

1. Livingston R.B. *Brain mechanisms in conditioning and learning.* Neurosciences Research Program Bulletin. Pg. 349–354. 1966.
2. MediciNet. *Medical Definition of Neuroplasticity.* MediciNet. 2017.
   http://www.medicinenet.com/script/main/art.asp?articlekey=40362
3. Rakic, P. *Neurogenesis in adult primate neocortex: an evaluation of the evidence.* Nature Reviews Neuroscience. 3 (1): 65–71. 2002.
4. Hampton, Debbie. *Neuroplasticity: The 10 Fundamentals Of Rewiring Your Brain.* Reset. 2015. http://reset.me/story/neuroplasticity-the-10-fundamentals-of-rewiring-your-brain/
5. Schwartz, Jeffrey. MD. *You Are Not Your Brain.* Avery. 2011.

4. Change Your Goal Mindset

1. Asatryan, Kira. *4 Disorders That May Thrive on Loneliness*. Psychology Today. 2015. https://www.psychologytoday.com/blog/the-art-closeness/201507/4-disorders-may-thrive-loneliness

5. Meditation

1. Lutz, A.; Greischar, L.L.; Rawlings, N.B.; Ricard, M.; Davidson, R. J. *Long-term meditators self-induce high-amplitude gamma synchrony during mental practice*. PNAS. 101 (46): 16369–73. PMC 526201Freely accessible. 2004.
2. Lazar, S. W., Kerr, C. E., Wasserman, R. H., Gray, J. R., Greve, D. N., Treadway, M. T., Benson, H. *Meditation experience is associated with increased cortical thickness*. Neuroreport, 16(17), 1893. 2005.
3. Kok, B. E., Waugh, C. E., & Fredrickson, B. L. *Meditation and health: The search for mechanisms of action. Social and Personality Psychology Compass,* 7(1), 27–39. 2013.
4. Zeidan, F., Johnson, S. K., Diamond, B. J., David, Z., & Goolkasian, P. *Mindfulness meditation improves cognition: Evidence of brief mental training*. 2010.